D0211847

No. IX.

The
Vellum-Parchment Shilling Series
OF
Miscellaneous Literature.

Field & Tuer,
Ye Leadenhalle Presse, E.C.

PRYOR PUBLICATIONS
WHITSTABLE AND WALSALL

Specialist in Facsimile Reproductions

MEMBER OF
INDEPENDENT PUBLISHERS GUILD

First Published circa 1880

Reprinted 1986, 1988, 1989, 1990 Twice, 1991 Twice, 1992,
1993, 1994, 1995, 1996, 1997 Fourth Imprint, 1998 Twice
1999 Twice, 2000

Over 160,000 copies of this edition sold to date
©1982 Pryor Publications

75 Dargate Road, Yorkletts, Whitstable,
Kent CT5 3AE, England.
Tel. & Fax: (01227) 274655
Email: alan@pryor-publish.clara.net
http://home.clara.net/pryor-publish
Kent Exporter of the Year Awards Winner 1998

ISBN 0 946014 02 7

A CIP Record for this book is available from the British Library

A full list of Titles sent free on request.

Printed and bound in Great Britain by
Thanet Press Limited, Margate, Kent

SECOND EDITION.

THE VELLUM-PARCHMENT SHILLING SERIES
OF MISCELLANEOUS LITERATURE.

Don't:

*A Manual of Mistakes & Improprieties more or
less prevalent in Conduct & Speech.*

"I'll view the manners of the town."—*Comedy of Errors.*

By CENSOR.

Unmutilated and Authorised Edition.

ONE SHILLING.

LONDON :
Field & Tuer, Yᵉ Leadenhalle Presse, E.C.
Simpkin, Marshall & Co.; Hamilton, Adams & Co.

FIELD & TUER,
YE LEADENHALLE PRESSE, E.C.
T. 3,239.

Preface.

(ENGLISH.)

———✦———

"*DON'T*" *tells us in a number of short epigrammatic sentences, each opening with an emphatic* DON'T, *what not to do in matters social. Written by an American for Americans of the better class,*[*] "DON'T" *has been very freely purchased*

———

[*] "*Don't wear evening dress in the morning.*" We may take it that possessors of swallow-tails and white ties are not found, even in America, amongst mechanics. In the preface it is stated that "*nearly every rule given is frequently violated by persons of at least good social standing.*"

on the other side. As a guide to the usages of polite society, the educated English reader will learn nothing from its pages, but, reading between the lines, he will be much amused and astonished. The Author of " Don't *" is a gentleman, and writes with a gentleman's instincts. To English readers, his "* Don'ts *" admit a flood of daylight behind the scenes of Transatlantic social life. They will learn for the first time that there are Americans in a good position who appear at table in their dressing-gown and slippers, or shirt-sleeves; and ladies—they are warned, by the way, not to wear their diamonds in the morning—who habitually forget to remove their curl papers before appearing at the breakfast table. Spitting upon the carpet naturally comes in for severe condemnation; and the authority of Dr. Wendell Holmes seems necessary to prove that a handkerchief should be used in blowing one's nose.**

*It will be noticed that the Author of "*Don't*," who naturally relies on the usages of the older country, is not always a safe guide; and, moreover, is a little inclined to obstinacy. He is at some pains to prove that in sending one's plate for a second helping of food, the knife and fork should be kept back; and if his dictum be not accepted, he gravely proposes as a compromise that the fork should be left on the plate and the knife kept back; and he is equally astray when he indicates the table instead of the chair as the proper place to leave one's napkin. Of errors peculiarly American, "*Don't*" is the advice given in the use of* du *for* do*—* "du tell;" *rowt for* route; *tower for* tour; *rubbers or* gums *for* overshoes; *sick for*

---

* *"Critics may condemn some of the injunctions as over-nice!"*—Vide (American) Preface.

unwell; elegant *for fine*—" an elegant morning," "an elegant piece of beef;" despise *for dislike*—" I despise turnips;" I guess *for I think; and so on.*

Of errors equally prevalent at home, some of us, even with handles to our names, may be warned against the slip-shod habit of dropping the final g. " *Don't say* comin' goin', singin', *for coming, going, singing;" and for a richly-deserved scourge for middle-class English backs, read this:* " Don't, as hostess, follow the English fashion, and omit napkins at breakfast. The hardihood with which an Englishman attacks coffee and eggs without a napkin may excite our wonder; but how can the practice be defended? Is it anything less than disgusting?"

CENSOR.

London.

Preface.

(AMERICAN.)

*I*T so happens that most of the rules of society are prohibitory in character. This fact suggested the negative form adopted in this little book, and permitted the various injunctions to be expressed in a sententious and emphatic manner.

Many of the rules here given are necessarily drawn from established authorities, but a considerable number of them are the result of the compiler's personal observation and experience.

There are some persons, no doubt, who will condemn many things here said as unnecessary, because generally known. It was necessary to include familiar rules in order to give completeness to the list; but any one who carefully observes will find that nearly every rule given is frequently violated by persons of at least good social standing.

Other critics may condemn some of the injunctions as over-nice. All that can be said to these persons is, that every one has the lawful right to determine for himself at what point below the highest point he is content to let his social culture stop.

The plan of the book does not include questions of etiquette, except incidentally. There are various volumes that set forth all the details of receiving visitors and making visits, of parties, of dinners, of card sending and receiving, etc., to which those interested are referred.

CENSOR.

New York.

Contents.

Don't.

I.

At Table.*

DON'T, as an invited guest, be late to dinner. This is a wrong to your host, to other guests, and to the dinner.

Don't be late at the domestic table, as this is a wrong to your family, and is not calculated to promote harmony and good feeling.

* The greater number of these directions apply to all occasions and to all persons, but some have reference to special times, others to guests only or to hosts only.

Don't seat yourself until the ladies are seated, or, at a dinner-party, until your host or hostess gives the signal. Don't introduce, if you introduce at all, after the company is seated.

Don't sit a foot off from the table, or sit jammed up against it.

Don't tuck your napkin under your chin, or spread it upon your breast. Bibs and tuckers are for the nursery. Don't spread your napkin over your lap; let it fall over your knee.

Don't serve gentlemen guests at your table before *all* the ladies are served, including those who are members of your own household.

Don't eat soup from the end of the spoon, but from the side. Don't gurgle, or draw in your breath, or make other noises when eating soup. Don't ask for a second service of soup.

Don't bend over your plate, or drop your head to get each mouthful. Keep an upright attitude as nearly as you can without being stiff.

Don't bite your bread. Break it off. Don't break your bread into your soup.

Don't eat with your knife. Never put your knife into your mouth. (Is this advice unnecessary? Go into any restaurant and observe.) Don't load up the fork with food with your knife, and then cart it, as it were, to your mouth. Take up on the fork what it can easily carry, and no more.

Don't use a steel knife with fish. A silver knife is now placed by the side of each plate for the fish course.

Don't handle fork or knife awkwardly. Let the handles of both knife and fork rest in the palm of the hand. How to handle knife and fork well can be acquired only by observation and practice. Don't stab with the fork, or handle it as if it were a dagger. Always carry food to the mouth with an inward curve of the fork or spoon.

Don't eat fast, or gorge. Take always plenty of time. Haste is vulgar.

Don't fill your mouth with too much food, and don't masticate audibly. Eat gently and quietly and easily.

Don't put your knife into the butter, into the salt-cellar, or into any dish.

Don't spread out your elbows when you are cutting your meat. Keep your elbows close to your side.

Don't, when you drink, elevate your glass as if you were going to stand it inverted on your nose, as some do. Bring the glass perpendicularly to the lips, and then lift it to a slight angle. Do this easily.

Don't eat vegetables with a spoon. Eat them with a fork. The rule is not to eat anything with a spoon that can be eaten with a fork. Even ices are now often eaten with a fork.

Don't devour the last mouthful of soup, the last fragment of bread, the last morsel of food. It is not expected that your plate should be sent away cleansed by your gastronomic exertions.

Don't leave your knife and fork on your plate when you send it for a second supply.*

* This rule is disputed. One of my critics affirms that the best English usage is exactly the contrary. I have before me directions written by Lord Cholmondeley, a leader

c

Don't reject bits of bone, or other substances,
    by spitting them back into the plate.   Qui-

of fashion in London a generation or two ago, in which he
says, " Be sure never to send your knife and fork when you
send your plate to be served a second time."   This was
written, it is true, a long time ago, but is it likely that English custom can now be directly reversed?   The logic of
the question proves the correctness of the rule.   It is not
at all easy to place food on a plate already occupied by a
knife and fork, and hence to send a plate thus encumbered
is to put an obstacle in the way of your host, or whoever
acts as carver—and it is a law of politeness to always incommode one's self rather than incommode others.   It is
asked, What shall one do with his knife and fork?   The
handles of knives and forks are now always loaded, hence
they can rest on the table without the blades or tines touch-
ing the cloth ; or one may, with a little skill, hold his knife
and fork in his hands without awkwardness.   If one can
not manage to do this, then here is a compromise : let the
fork remain on the plate, as that alone would be a very
slight obstruction, while the sender could without awkwardness retain the knife, one article being easier to
manage than two.

etly eject them upon your fork, holding it
to your lips, and then place them on the
plate. Fruit-stones may be removed by the
fingers.

Don't stretch across another's plate in order
to reach anything.

Don't apply to your neighbour to pass articles
when the servant is at hand.

Don't finger articles; don't play with your
napkin, or your goblet, or your fork, or with
anything.

Don't mop your face or beard with your napkin. Draw it across your lips neatly.

Don't turn your back to one person for the
purpose of talking to another; don't talk
across the one seated next to you.

Don't forget that the lady sitting at your side
has the first claim upon your attention. A

lady at your side should not be neglected, whether you have been introduced to her or not.

Don't talk when your mouth is full—never, in fact, have your mouth full. It is more healthful and in better taste to eat by small morsels.

Don't be embarrassed. Endeavor to be self-possessed and at ease; to accomplish which, try and not be self-conscious. Remember that self-respect is as much a virtue as respect for others.

Don't drop your knife or fork; but, if you do, don't be disconcerted. Quietly ask the servant for another, and give the incident no further heed. Don't be disquieted at accidents or blunders of any kind, but let all mishaps pass off without comment and with philosophical indifference.

Don't throw yourself loungingly back in your chair. The Romans lounged at table, but modern civilization does not permit it.

Don't rest your elbows on the table; don't lean on the table.

Don't use a toothpick at table, unless it is necessary; in that case, cover your mouth with one hand while you remove the obstruction that troubles you.

Don't eat onions or garlic, unless you are dining alone, and intend to remain alone some hours thereafter. One should not wish to carry with him unpleasant evidences of what he has been eating or drinking.

Don't press food upon a guest. This once was thought necessary, and it was also considered polite for a guest to continue accepting, or to signify by a particular sign that

he had enough.* To worry a guest with
ceaseless importunities is now considered in
the worst possible taste.

Don't, as guest, fold your napkin when you
have finished. Place the napkin loosely on
the table.

Don't fail, at dinner, to rise when the ladies
leave the table. Remain standing until they
have left the room, and then reseat yourself,
if you intend to remain for cigars.

---

*McMaster tells us that the Prince of Broglie, " who
traveled in our country in 1782, relates, in one of his letters,
that he was invited to dine with the lady of Robert Morris;
that he went; that he was repeatedly asked to have his cup
refilled ; that he consented ; and that, when he had swal-
lowed the twelfth cup of tea, his neighbor whispered in his
ear and told him when he had had enough of the water
diet he should place his spoon across his cup, else the hostess would go on urging him to drink tea till the crack of
doom."

Don't make a pronounced attempt at correctness of manner; don't be vulgar, but don't, on the other hand, show that you are trying hard not to be vulgar. It is better to make mistakes than to be obviously struggling not to make them.

Don't drink too much wine.

Don't thank host or hostess for your dinner. Express pleasure in the entertainment, when you depart—that is all.

Don't come to breakfast in *deshabille*. A lady's morning toilet should be simple, but fresh and tasteful, and her hair *not* in curl-papers. A gentleman should wear his morning suit, and never his dressing-gown. There are men who sit at table in their shirt-sleeves. This is very vulgar.

Don't, as hostess, follow the English fashion

and omit napkins at breakfast. The hardihood with which an Englishman attacks coffee and eggs without a napkin may excite our wonder, but how can the practice be defended ? Is it anything less than disgusting ?

Don't drink from your saucer. While you must avoid this vulgarity, don't take notice of it, or of any mistake of the kind, when committed by others. It is related that at the table of an English prince a rustic guest poured his tea into his saucer, much to the visible amusement of the court ladies and gentlemen present. Whereupon the prince quietly poured his own tea into his saucer, thereby rebuking his ill-mannered court, and putting his guest in countenance.

Don't carry your spoon in your tea or coffee cup; this habit is the cause frequently of one upsetting the cup. Let the spoon lie in the saucer.

Don't smear a slice of bread with butter; break it into small pieces, and then butter.

Don't break an egg into a cup or glass, but eat it always from the shell.*

Don't read newspaper or book or letters at table, if others are seated with you.

Don't decorate your shirt-front with egg or coffee drippings, and don't ornament your coat-lapels with grease-spots. A little care will prevent these accidents. Few things are more distasteful than to see a gentleman

* This rule is not generally observed with us, but it is universal in England, where an egg beaten up in a glass is considered an unpleasant mess. Refined usage here accords with the English.

bearing upon his apparel ocular evidence of having breakfasted or dined.

Don't rise from the table until the meal is finished.

Many rules of the table seem to some persons very arbitrary, no doubt, but they are the result of the mature experience of society, and, however trivial they may appear to be, there is always some good reason for them. The object of a code is to exclude or prevent everything that is disagreeable, and to establish the best method of doing that which is to be done. It is not necessary to point out that a dinner served and eaten in disregard of all rules would be a savage carousal ; this being true, it ought to be seen that, if rules in any degree elevate the act of eating, then a code of rules generally observed lifts eating to a still higher plane, and makes it a fine art.

II.

In Dress and Personal Habits.

DON'T neglect personal cleanliness—which is
more neglected than careless observers suppose.

Don't wear soiled linen. Be scrupulously particular on this point.

Don't be untidy in anything. Neatness is
one of the most important of the minor
morals.

Don't neglect the details of the toilet. Many
persons, neat in other particulars, carry
blackened finger-nails. This is disgusting.

Don't neglect the small hairs that project from the nostrils and grow about the apertures of the ears—small matters of the toilet often overlooked.

Don't cleanse your ears, or your nose, or trim and clean your finger-nails, in public. Cleanliness and neatness in all things pertaining to the person are indispensable, but toilet offices are proper in the privacy of one's apartment only.

Don't use hair-dye. The color is not like nature, and deceives no one.*

* Hair and beard dyed black produce a singular effect. They seem to coarsen and vulgarize the lines of the face. Any one who has ever seen an elderly gentleman suddenly abandon his dye, and appear with his gray locks in all their natural beauty, will realize what we mean—for he has seen what appeared to him a rather coarse and sensuous face all at once changed into one of refinement and character.

Don't use hair-oil or pomades. This habit was once quite general, but it is now considered vulgar, and it is certainly not cleanly.

Don't wear apparel with decided colors or with pronounced patterns. Don't—we address here the male reader—wear anything that is *pretty*. What have men to do with pretty things? Select quiet colors and unobtrusive patterns, and adopt no style of cutting that belittles the figure. It is right enough that men's apparel should be becoming, that it should be graceful, and that it should lend dignity to the figure; but it should never be ornamental, capricious, or pretty.

Don't wear fancy-colored shirts, or embroidered shirt-fronts. Spotted or otherwise decorated shirts are fashionable in summer, but the taste is questionable.   White, plain linen is always in better taste.

Don't wear evening dress in the morning, or on any occasion before six o'clock dinner.

Don't wear black broadcloth in the morning; or, at least, don't wear black broadcloth trousers except for evening dress.

Don't wear your hat cocked over your eye, or thrust back upon your head. One method is rowdyish, the other rustic.

Don't go with your boots unpolished; but don't have the polishing done in the public highways. A gentleman perched on a high curb-stone chair, within view of all passers-by, while he is having executed this finishing touch to his toilet, presents a picture more unique than dignified.

Don't wear trinkets, shirt-pins, finger-rings, or anything that is solely ornamental. One may wear shirt-studs, a scarf-pin, a watch-chain and a seal, because these articles are useful ; but the plainer they are the better.

Don't be a "swell" or a "dude," or whatever the fop of the period may be called.

Don't wear dressing-gown and slippers anywhere out of your bedroom. To appear at table or in any company in this garb is the very soul of vulgarity. It is equally vulgar to sit at table or appear in company in one's shirt sleeves.

Don't walk with a slouching, slovenly gait. Walk erectly and firmly, not stiffly ; walk with ease, but still with dignity. Don't bend out the knees, nor walk in-toed, nor drag your feet along ; walk in a large, easy, sim-

ple manner, without affectation but not neg-
ligently.

Don't carry your hands in your pockets.
Don't thrust your thumbs into the arm-holes
of your waistcoat.

Don't chew or nurse your toothpick in public
—or anywhere else. Don't use a toothpick,
except for a moment, to remove some obstacle ; and don't have the habit of sucking
your teeth.

Don't chew tobacco. It is a bad and ungentle-
manly habit. The neatest tobacco-chewer
can not wholly prevent the odor of tobacco
from affecting his breath and clinging to his
apparel, and the "places that know him"
are always redolent of the weed. If one
must chew, let him be particular where he
expectorates. He should not discharge to-

bacco-juice in public vehicles, on the side-walk, or in any place where it will be offensive.

Don't expectorate. Men in good health do not need to expectorate; with them continual expectoration is simply the result of habit. Men with bronchial or lung diseases are compelled to expectorate, but no one should discharge matter of the kind in public places except into vessels provided to receive it. Spitting upon the floor anywhere is inexcusable. One should not even spit upon the sidewalk, but go to the gutter for the purpose. One must not spit into the fire-place nor upon the carpet, and hence the English rule is for him to spit in his handkerchief—but this is not a pleasant alternative. On some occasions no other may offer.

Don't whistle in the street, in public vehicles, at public assemblies, or anywhere where it may annoy. Mem.: don't whistle at all.*

Don't laugh boisterously. Laugh heartily when the occasion calls for it, but the loud guffaw is not necessary to heartiness.

Don't have the habit of smiling or " grinning " at nothing. Smile or laugh when there is occasion to do either, but at other times keep your mouth shut and your manner com-

---

* Among the current nuisances, whistling is peculiarly obnoxious to some people. An anecdote is in circulation to the effect that a distinguished journalist and his son were in an omnibus, into which entered a man whistling loudly. Presently the journalist turned to his son and exclaimed in a loud voice, "Who is that lady whistling?" " It is not a lady, papa, it is a gentleman," answered the boy. " Oh, no, my son," was the reply, still in a loud voice, "that is impossible; no gentleman ever whistles in an omnibus." The whistler was silenced—it is to be hoped for ever.

posed.   People who laugh at everything are commonly capable of nothing.

Don't blow your nose in the presence of others if you can possibly avoid it.   Above all things, don't blow your nose with your fingers.   Dr. Oliver Wendell Holmes declares that, in all the discussions and differences of opinion as to what constitutes a gentleman, all disputants unite in excluding the man who blows his nose with his fingers.

Don't gape, or hiccough, or sneeze in company.   When there is an inclination to hiccough or sneeze, hold your breath for a moment and resist the desire, and you will find that it will pass off.

Don't have the habit of letting your lip drop and your mouth remain open.   "Shut your mouth," is the advice of a *savant*, who has

written a book on the subject. Breathe
through your nostrils and not through your
mouth ; sleep with your mouth closed ; keep
it closed except when you open it for a purpose. An open mouth indicates feebleness
of character, while the habit affects the teeth
and the general health.

Don't keep carrying your hands to your face,
pulling your whiskers, adjusting your hair,
or otherwise fingering yourself. Keep your
hands quiet and under control.

Don't be over-familiar. Don't strike your
friends on the back, nudge them in the side,
or give other physical manifestation of your
pleasure. Don't indulge in these familiari-
ties, or submit to them from others.

Don't bolt, without notice, into any one's private apartment. Respect always the pri-

vacy of your friends, however intimate you may be with them.

Don't wear your hat in a strictly private office. This is no more justifiable than wearing a hat in a drawing-room.

Don't carry a lighted cigar into a private office or into a salesroom. (See *Smoking*, under "In Public.")

Don't pick up letters, accounts, or anything of a private character that is lying on another's desk. Don't look over a person's shoulder when he is reading or writing.

Don't twirl a chair or other object while talking or listening to any one. This trick is very annoying and very common.

Don't beat a tattoo with your foot in company or anywhere, to the annoyance of others. Don't drum with your fingers on chair,

table, or window-pane.   Don't hum a tune.
The instinct for making noises is a survival
of savagery.

Don't be servile toward superiors, or arrogant
toward inferiors.   Maintain your dignity and
self-respect in one case, and exhibit a regard
for the feelings of people, whatever their
station may be, in the other.

Don't go into the presence of ladies with your
breath redolent of wine or spirits, or your
beard rank with the odor of tobacco.   Smok-
ers should be careful to wash the mustache
and beard after smoking.

Don't drink wine or spirits in the morning, or
often at other times than at dinner.   Don't
frequent bar-rooms.   Tippling is not only
vulgar and disreputable, but injurious to
health.

III.

In the Drawing-Room.

Don't, however brief your call, wear overcoat or overshoes into the drawing-room. If you are making a short call, carry your hat and cane in your hand, but never an umbrella.

Don't attempt to shake hands with everybody present. If hostess or host offers a hand, take it; a bow is sufficient for the rest.

Don't in any case, offer to shake hands with a lady. The initiative must always come from her. By the same principle don't offer

your hand to a person older than yourself,
or to any one whose rank may be supposed
to be higher than your own, until he has extended his.

Don't, as hostess, insist upon taking a caller's
hat or cane.   Pay no attention to these articles.
It is right that he should carry them ; it is
not right that you should notice them.

Don't be in a precipitate hurry to get into a
chair.   It is just as graceful, as easy, and as
proper, to stand ; and it is easier to converse
when in that attitude.

Don't be cold and distant ; don't, on the other
hand, be gushing and effusive.   A cordial
yet quiet manner is the best.

Don't stare at the furniture, at pictures, or at
other objects, and, of course, don't stare at
people present.

Don't fail to rise, if you are seated, whenever a lady enters the room.

Don't stretch yourself on the sofa, or in the easy-chair. Don't lounge anywhere except in your own apartment.

Don't sit cross-legged. Pretty nearly everybody of the male sex does—but, nevertheless, don't.

Don't sit with your chair resting on its hind legs. Keep quiet and at ease in your chair.

Don't keep shifting your feet about. Don't twirl your thumbs, or play with tassels or knobs, or other articles at hand. Cultivate repose.

Don't be self-conscious. " True politeness," says a writer, " is always so busy in thinking of others that it has no time to think of itself."

Don't, in introducing, present ladies to gentlemen ; gentlemen, whatever their rank, should
be presented to ladies. Young men should
be presented to elderly men, and not the reverse; young women to elderly women.

Don't, if you are asked to play or sing, refuse
unless you really intend not to perform. To
refuse, simply in order to lead your hostess
on to repeated importunities, is an intolerable exhibition of vanity and caprice. To
every hostess, therefore, we say :

Don't ask any one more than once after a first
refusal to sing or play. A first refusal may
arise from modesty or hesitation, but a second
should be considered final.

Don't touch people when you have occasion
to address them. Catching people by the
arms or the shoulders, or nudging them to

attract their attention, is a violation of good breeding.

Don't talk over-loud, or try to monopolize the conversation.

Don't talk to one person across another.

Don't whisper in company. If what you wish to say can not be spoken aloud, reserve it for a suitable occasion.

Don't talk about yourself or your affairs. If you wish to be popular, talk to people about what interests them, not about what interests you.

Don't talk in a social circle to one person of the company about matters that solely concern him and yourself, or which you and he alone understand.

Don't talk about your maladies, or about your afflictions of any kind. Complaining people are pronounced on all hands great bores.

Don't talk about people that are unknown to those present.

Don't be witty at another's expense; don't ridicule any one; don't infringe in any way the harmony of the company.

Don't repeat the scandals and malicious rumors of the hour.

Don't discuss equivocal people, nor broach topics of questionable propriety.

Don't dwell on the beauty of women not present; on the splendor of other people's houses; on the success of other people's entertainments; on the superiority of anybody. Excessive praise of people or things elsewhere implies discontent with people or things present.

Don't fail to exercise tact. If you have not tact, you at least can think first about others and next about yourself, and this will go a good way toward it.

Don't introduce religious or political topics. Discussions on these subjects are very apt to cause irritation, and hence it is best to avoid them.

Don't give a false coloring to your statements. Truthfulness is largely a matter of habit. Where very few people would deceive or lie maliciously, many become wholly untrustworthy on account of their habit of exaggeration and false coloring.

Don't interrupt. To cut one short in the middle of his story is unpardonable.

Don't contradict. Difference of opinion is no cause of offense, but downright contradiction is a violation of one of the canons of good society.

Don't be disputatious. An argument which goes rapidly from one to another may be tolerated; but when two people in company fall into a heated dispute, to the exclusion of all other topics, the hostess should arbitrarily interfere and banish the theme.

Don't be long-winded. When you have a story to tell, do not go into every detail and branch off at every word—be direct, compact, clear, and get to the point as soon as you can.

Don't cling to one subject; don't talk about matters that people generally are not interested in; don't, in short, be a bore.

Don't repeat old jokes or tell time-worn stories. Don't make obvious puns. An occasional pun, if a good one, is a good thing; but a ceaseless flow of puns is simply maddening.

Don't repeat anecdotes, good or bad. A very good thing becomes foolishness to the ears of the listener after hearing it several times.

Don't respond to remarks made to you with mere monosyllables. This is chilling, if not fairly insulting. Have something to say, and say it.

Don't appear listless and indifferent, or exhibit impatience when others are talking. Listening politely to every one is a cardinal necessity of good breeding.

Don't be conceited. Don't dilate on your own acquirements or achievements; don't expatiate on what you have done or are going to do, or on your superior talents in anything.

Don't always make yourself the hero of your own stories.

Don't show a disposition to find fault or depreciate. Indiscriminate praise is nauseating; but, on the other hand, indiscriminate condemnation is irritating. A man of the world should have good appreciation and good depreciation—that is, a keen sense of the merits of a thing, and an equally keen sense of its faults.

Don't be sulky because you imagine yourself neglected. Think only of pleasing; and try to please. You will end by being pleased.

Don't show repugnance even to a bore. A supreme test of politeness is submission to various social inflictions without a wince.

Don't, when at the card-table, moisten your thumb and fingers at your lips in order to facilitate the dealing of the cards. This common habit is very vulgar. The aristocratic circles of a European court were much horrified a few years ago by the practice of this trick by the American embassador.

Don't show ill-temper, if the game goes against you.

Don't fail in proper attention to elderly people Young persons are often scandalously neglectful of the aged, especially if they are deaf or otherwise afflicted. Nothing shows a better heart, or a nicer sense of true politeness, than kindly attention to those advanced in years.

Don't in company open a book and begin reading to yourself. If you are tired of the company, withdraw; if not, honor it with your attention.

Don't stand before the fire, to the exclusion of
the warmth from others. Don't forget good
manners in anything.

Don't, in entering or leaving a room with
ladies, go before them. They should have
precedence always.

Don't keep looking at your watch, as if you
were impatient for the time to pass.

Don't wear out your welcome by too long a
stay ; on the other hand, don't break up the
company by a premature departure. A little
observation and good sense will enable you
to detect the right time to say " Good-
night."

IV.

In Public.

DON'T neglect to keep to the right of the promenade, otherwise there may be collisions and much confusion.

Don't brush against people, or elbow people, or in any way show disregard for others.

Don't fail to apologize if you tread upon or stumble against any one, or if you inconvenience one in any way. Be considerate and polite always.

Don't stare at people, or laugh at any peculiarity of manner or dress. Don't point at persons or objects. Don't turn and look after people that have passed. Don't forget to be a gentleman.

Don't carry cane or umbrella in a crowd horizontally. This trick is a very annoying one to the victims of it.

Don't smoke in the street, unless in unfrequented avenues. Don't smoke in public vehicles. Don't smoke in any place where it is likely to be offensive. Wherever you do indulge in a cigar, don't puff smoke into the face of any one, man or woman.

Don't expectorate on the sidewalk. Go to the curb-stone and discharge the saliva into the gutter. Men who eject great streams of tobacco-juice on the sidewalk, or on the floors of public vehicles, ought to be driven out of civilized society.

Don't eat fruit or anything else in the public
streets. A gentleman on the promenade, en-
gaged in munching an apple or a pear, presents a more amusing than edifying picture.

Don't obstruct the entrance to churches, the-
atres, or assemblies. Don't stand before ho-
tels or other places and stare at passers-by.
This is a most idle and insolent habit.

Don't stop acquaintances and stand in the cen-
ter of the sidewalk, forcing every one out of
his path. On such occasions draw your acquaintance one side.

Don't stand on car-platforms, thereby prevent-
ing the easy ingress and egress of passengers.
Remember the rights and the comfort of
others.

Don't forget to raise your hat to every lady
acquaintance you meet, and to every gentle-

man you salute, when he is accompanied by
a lady, whether you know her or not ; and
when with an acquaintance raise your hat
when he does so, though you may not know
the lady he salutes.

Don't stop your lady acquaintances in the
street if you wish to speak to them ; turn
and walk by their side, and leave them with
raised hat when you have done.

Don't remove your glove when you wish to
shake hands, or apologize for not doing so.
It is proper to offer the hand gloved.

Don't neglect to raise your hat to a strange
lady if you have occasion to address her.
If she drops her handkerchief, and you pick
it up for her, raise your hat. If in an omnibus you pass her fare to the conductor, raise
your hat. Every little service of the kind

should be accompanied by a distant, respectful salutation.

Don't be in haste to introduce. Be sure that it is mutually desired before presenting one person to another.

Don't, in a walk, introduce your companion to every person you may chance to meet. Offhand street introductions are rarely called for, and commonly serve no end.*

Don't ask questions of strangers indiscriminately. Young women run risks in approaching unknown people with questions, and they should scrupulously avoid doing so. In traveling, inquire of the conductor or

---

* "It is the bane of social life in America," says a correspondent, "that you are continually being introduced to people about whom you care nothing and whom you do not care to know, unless you are a bagman, a railway-conductor, or a reporter."

of some official ; in the street, wait until a policeman can be found.

Don't be over-civil. Do not let your civility fall short, but over-civility is a mistake. Don't rush to pick up a man's hat ; don't pick up any article that a stranger or companion may drop, unless there are special reasons for doing so. Be prompt to pick up anything that a lady lets fall, and extend this politeness to elderly or infirm men. But haste to wait on equals is over-civility ; it has a touch of servility, and is not sanctioned by the best usage.

Don't rush for a seat in a car or at a public entertainment, in utter disregard of every one else, pushing rudely by women and children, hustling men who are older or less active, and disregarding every law of polite-

ness. If one should, on an occasion of this
kind, lose his seat in consequence of a little
polite consideration, he would have the con-
solation of standing much higher in his own
esteem—which is something.

Don't occupy more space in an omnibus or car
than you require. In this particular women
are greater sinners than men. One who has
traveled a good deal in local vehicles declares
that he has ascertained the exact arithmetical
ratio of the sexes, which is as six to five—for,
in an omnibus, a seat that will hold six men
never accommodates more than five women.

Don't enter a crowded omnibus or street-car.
There doubtless are occasions when one can
not well help doing so, but many times the
vehicle that follows will afford plenty of
room. A person who enters a crowded

public vehicle is an intruder, and has no
rights that anybody is bound to respect.*

* The manners of the people in public vehicles seem
daily to be growing worse, and, if they continue to decline,
it will become almost impossible for ladies, at least, if not
gentlemen, to enter them.   The first thing one encounters
when he attempts to take a car, is a cad lazily lounging
against the platform-rail, with his legs stretched out, so
that, unless you are alert, you stumble over him, while, perhaps, a puff of smoke is blown in your face.   Such a fellow
should be promptly lodged in the street ; but he seems to
be under the protection of the conductor, an official whose
apparent business it is to give moral support to all the
loafers that take pleasure in inconveniencing travelers. One
is scarcely within the car ere he is tripped up by another
man's extended legs ; and, if the occupants are few enough,
or compliant enough, to enable him to get a seat, he may
find himself by the side of a fellow who is industriously
making a pool of tobacco-juice on the floor before him.   It
is amazing that such a thing should be tolerated ; but ladies
make no open protest, gentlemen are heedless, the conduct-
or is complacent, and the brute remains undisturbed, although he has no more right to empty this matter in a pub-

Don't bustle into a theatre or concert after
the performance has begun, to the annoyance of others. Arrive early and be seated
in time. The manager who will resolutely
refuse permission for any one to enter
an auditorium after the curtain has risen,
will win for himself a golden meed of
praise.

Don't talk at the theatre or at a concert when
the performance is going on. To disturb
others who wish to listen is gross ill breeding ; but, unfortunately, it is common with

lic vehicle than any other kind of filth. Ere one has left the
car the conductor has probably rudely seized him by the
shoulders in demanding his fare ; he has been compelled to
listen to idiotic whistlers and other noise-makers ; and his
emergence from the vehicle has been accomplished only
after a struggle with the boors that congregate on the plat-
form.

the very class who pretend to an exclusive
share of good breeding.

Don't at any public entertainment make a move
to leave the auditorium before the performance is over.   Men who recklessly and self-
ishly disturb public assemblies in this way
have the instincts of savages, not of gentlemen.

V.

In Speech.

Don't speak ungrammatically. Study books of grammar, and the writings of the best authors.

Don't pronounce incorrectly. Listen carefully to the conversation of cultivated people, and consult the dictionaries.

Don't mangle your words, or smother them, or swallow them. Speak with a distinct enunciation.

Don't talk in a high, shrill voice, and avoid nasal tones. Cultivate a chest-voice; learn to moderate your tones. Talk always in a low register, but not too low.

Don't use slang. There is some slang that, according to Thackeray, is gentlemanly slang, and other slang that is vulgar. If one does not know the difference, let him avoid slang altogether, and then he will be safe.

Don't use profane language. Don't multiply epithets and adjectives; don't be too fond of superlatives. Moderate your transports.

Don't use meaningless exclamations, such as "Oh, my!" "Oh, crackey!" etc.

Don't interject *sir* or *madam* freely into your conversation. Never say *ma'am* at all. Young people should be taught to say "Yes, papa," "No, mamma" (with accent on the second syllable of *mamma* and *papa*), "Yes, uncle,"

"No, aunt," and so on, instead of always "Yes, sir," "No, ma'am," etc. *Sir* is right toward superiors, but it must even in this case be sparingly used.

Don't address a young lady as *miss*. Don't say "Miss Mary," "Miss Susan." This strictly is permissible with servants only. Address young ladies by their surname, with prefix of *miss*, except when in a family of sisters a distinction must be made, and then give the name in full.

Don't clip final consonants. Don't say *comin'*, *goin'*, *singin'*, for *coming, going, singing*. Don't say *an'* for *and*.

Don't mispronounce vowel-sounds in unaccented syllables. Don't say *persition* for *position*, *pertater* for *potato*, *sentunce* for *sentence*. On the other hand, don't lay too much stress

In Speech.

on these sounds—touch them lightly but correctly.

Don't say *ketch* for *catch*, or *ken* for *can*. Don't say *feller* for *fellow*, or *winder* for *window*, or *meller* for *mellow*, or *to-morrer* for *to-morrow.* Don't imagine that ignoramuses only make these mistakes. They are often through carelessness made by people of some education. Don't, therefore, be careless in these little points.

Don't say *secatary* for *secretary*, or *sal'ry* for *salary*. Don't say *hist'ry* for *history*.

Don't say *doo* for *dew* or *due*. Don't say *dooty* for *duty*. Remember to give the diphthongal sound of *eu* wherever it belongs. The perversity of pronunciation in this particular is singular. "A heavy *doo* fell last night," one rustic will say. "*Du* tell!" will come as a response from another.

Don't drop the sound of *r* where it belongs, as *ahm* for *arm, wahm* for *warm, hoss* for *horse, govahment* for *government.* The omission of *r* in these and similar words—usually when it falls after a vowel—is very common.

Don't pronounce *route* as if it were written *rowt ;* it should be like *root.* Don't, also, pronounce *tour* as if you were speaking of a tower. Let it be pronounced as if it were *toor.*

Don't pronounce *calm* and *palm* as if they rhymed with *ham.* Give the *a* the broad sound, as in *father.*

Don't say *gents* for *gentlemen,* nor *pants* for *pantaloons.* These are inexcusable vulgarisms. Don't say *vest* for *waistcoat.*

F

Don't say *party* for *person*. This is abominable, and yet very common.

Don't say *lady* when you mean wife.

Don't say "right away," if you wish to avoid Americanisms. Say *immediately* or *directly*.

Don't say *rubbers* or *gums*. Say *overshoes*. Why should the material of an article of clothing be mentioned?

Don't say *female* for *woman*. A sow is a female; a mare is a female. The female sex of the human kind is entitled to some distinctive term.

Don't say *sick* except when nausea is meant. Say *ill, unwell, indisposed*.

Don't say *posted* for *well informed*. Don't say *balance* for *remainder*. Don't use trade terms except for trade purposes.

Don't say, "Have the cars come in?" Say, "Has the train come in?" It is better to travel by *rail* than by *cars*. These are simply preferences—matters of taste merely.

Don't call your servants *girls*. Call the cook *cook*, and the nurse *nurse*, and the house-maids *maids*.

Don't use wrong adjectives. There is perhaps no adjective so misused as *elegant*. Don't say "an elegant morning," or an "elegant piece of beef," or "an elegant scene," or "an elegant picture." This word has been so vulgarized by misuse that it is better not to use it at all.

Don't use extravagant adjectives. Don't say *magnificent* when a thing is merely pretty, or *splendid* when *excellent* or some other word will do. Extravagance of this kind is never in good taste.

Don't use the words *hate* and *despise* to express mere dislikes. The young lady who declares that she "hates yellow ribbons" and "despises turnips," may have sound principles, but she evinces a great want of discrimination in the selection of epithets.

Don't say *hung* when *hanged* is meant. Men, unfortunately, are sometimes hanged; pictures are hung.

Don't say that anybody or anything is *genteel*. Don't use the word at all. Say a person is "well bred," or a thing is "tasteful."

Don't say *transpire* when you mean *occur*. *Transpire* means to become known, and hence is erroneously used in the sense of taking place.

Don't say *yeh* for *yes;* and don't imitate the English *ya-as.* Don't respond to a remark with a prolonged exclamatory and interrogative *ye-es.* This is a rank Yankeeism.

Don't say *don't* for *does not. Don't* is a contraction of *do not,* not of *does not.* Hence, "he don't" is not permissible. Say "He doesn't," or use the words in full.

Don't say *ain't* for *isn't,* and, above all, don't say *'tain't.* Say *aren't* for *are not, isn't* for *is not;* and, although *ain't* may by a stretch be considered an abbreviation of "am not." it is in better taste to speak the words in full.

Don't say " I *done* it," "he *done* it," "they *done* it." This is a very gross error, yet it is often made by people who ought to know better. "I did it," "he did it," "they did it," is, it ought to be unnecessary to say, the correct form.

Don't say "I *seen*," say "I *saw*." This error is commonly made by the same people who say "I *done* it." A similar error is, "If he had *went*," instead of "If he had *gone*."

Don't say "It is *him*," say "It is *he*." So, also, "It is *I*," not "It is *me*"; "It is *they*," not "It is *them*."

Don't say "He is older than *me*," say "He is older than *I*." "I am taller than *he*," not "I am taller than *him*."

Don't say "Charles and me are going to church." The proper form is, "Charles and *I* are going," etc.

Don't say "Between you and *I*." By an ingenious perversity, the same people who insist, in the instances we have cited, upon using the objective case where the nominative is called for, in this phrase reverse the proceeding. They should say, "Between you and *me*."

Don't, in referring to a person, say *he* or *she* or *him*, but always mention the name. "Mrs. Smith thinks it will rain," not "*she* thinks it will rain." There are men who continually refer to their wives as *she*, and wives who have commonly no other name than *he* for their husbands. This is abominable.

Don't say *lay* for *lie*. It is true, Byron committed this blunder—"There let him *lay*"—but poets are not always safe guides. *Lay* expresses transitive action ; *lie* expresses rest "I will *lie* down" ; "I will *lay* it down."

Don't use *them* for *those*. "*Them* boots," "*them* bonnets," etc., is so gross an error that we

commonly hear it only from the uneducated.

Don't say, "I am *through*," when you are an-
nouncing that you have finished dinner or
breakfast. "Are you through?" asked an
American of an Englishman when seated at
table. "Through!" exclaimed the Englishman, looking in an alarmed way down to
the floor and up to the ceiling—"through
what?"

Don't misuse the words *lady* and *gentleman*.
Don't say "A nice lady." If you must use
the word *nice*, say "A nice woman." Don't
say "A pleasant gentleman," say "An agree-
able person." Say "What kind of man is
he?" not "What kind of gentleman is he?"
Say "She is a good woman," not "a good
lady." The indiscriminate use of *lady* and

gentleman indicates want of culture. These terms should never be used when sex pure and simple is meant.

Don't say "I *guess*" for "I *think*," or "I *expect*" for "I *suppose*."

Don't use *plenty* as an adjective, but say *plentiful.* So say the purists, although old writers frequently violated this rule. "If reasons were as *plenty* as blackberries," says Falstaff. If we obey the rule, we must say "money is *plentiful*," not "money is *plenty*."

Don't use the word *please* too much. Say, "Will you kindly oblige me," or something equivalent.

Don't fall into the habit of repeating worn-out proverbs and over-used quotations. It becomes not a little irritating to have to listen to one who ceaselessly applies or misap-

plies a threadbare stock of " wise saws " and
stupid sayings.

Don't use *fix* in the sense of putting in order,
setting to rights, etc. This is a condemned
Americanism. *Fix* means to make fast, to
permanently set in place, and hence the common American usage is peculiarly wrong.

Don't adopt the common habit of calling
everything *funny* that chances to be a little
odd or strange. *Funny* can only be rightly
use when the comical is meant.

Don't use *mad* for *angry*. This has been de-
nounced as peculiarly an Americanism, and
it *is* an Americanism so far as current usage
goes ; but the word is employed in this sense
in the New Testament, it is occasionally
found in old English authors, and, according
to articles recently published in the London

"Athenæum," it is not uncommon in certain
out-of-the-way places in England.

Don't use a plural pronoun when a singular is
called for. "Every passenger must show *their*
ticket," illustrates a prevalent error. "Everybody put on *their* hats" is another instance.
It should be, "Everybody put on *his* hat."

Don't say "blame it on him," but simply,
"blame him." The first form is common
among the uneducated.

Don't use *got* where it is unnecessary. "I
have *got* an umbrella" is a common form of
speech, but *got* here is needless, and it is far
from being a pleasing word. "I have a
book," not "I have *got* a book," and so in all
similar cases.

Don't use *less* for *fewer* in referring to things
of numbers. *Less* should be applied to

bulk only; "*less* than a bushel, *fewer* than a hundred," indicates the proper distinction to be made in the use of the two words.

Don't use *quantity* for *number*. "A quantity of wheat" is right enough, but what are we to think of the phrase, "a quantity of people"?

Don't use adjectives when adverbs are required. Don't say, for instance, "This pear is *uncommon* good," but, "This pear is *uncommonly* good." For rules on the use of adverbs consult books on grammar.

Don't say "awfully nice," "awfully pretty," etc.; and don't accumulate bad grammar upon bad taste by saying "awful nice." Use the word *awful* with a sense of its correct meaning.

Don't say "loads of time" or "oceans of time." There is no meaning to these phrases. Say "ample time" or "time enough."

Don't say "lots of things," meaning an "abundance of things." A *lot* of anything means a separate portion, a part allotted. *Lot* for *quantity* is an Americanism.

Don't say that "the health of the President was *drank*," or that "the race was *ran*." For *drank* say *drunk;* for *ran* say *run.*

Don't use *smart* to express cleverness, brightness, or capability. This use of the word is very common, but it is not sanctioned by people of the best taste.

Don't habitually use the word *folks*—"his folks," "our folks," "their folks," etc. Strictly, the word should be *folk*, the plural form being a corruption ; but, while usage sanc-

tions *folks* for *folk*, it is in better taste not
to use the word at all.

Don't speak of this or that kind of food being
healthy or *unhealthy*; say always *wholesome*
or *unwholesome*.

Don't say *learn* for *teach*. It is not right to
say "will *learn* them what to do," but "will
teach them what to do." The teacher can
only teach; the pupil must learn.

Don't say *donate* when you mean *give*. The
use of this pretentious word for every instance of giving has become so common as
to be fairly nauseating. Good, plain, vigor-
ous Saxon is never nauseating. If one can
not give his church or town library a little
money without calling it *donating*, let him,
in the name of good English, keep his gift
until he has learned better.

Don't pronounce *God* as if it were written *gawd*, or *dog* as if it were *dorg*. In each case *o* should have the short sound, the first word rhyming with *rod*, the second with *log*.

Don't say *ruther* for *rather*. Pronounce *rather* to rhyme with *father*.

Don't use *admire* for *like*. "I should admire to go with you" is neither good English nor good sense.

Don't notice in others a slip of grammar or a mispronunciation in a way to cause a blush or to offend. If you refer to anything of the kind, do it courteously, and not in the hearing of other persons.

VI.

In General.

DON'T conduct correspondence on postal-
cards. A brief business message on a postal-
card is not out of the way, but a private
communication on an open card is almost
insulting to your correspondent. It is
questionable whether a note on a postal-
card is entitled to the courtesy of a response.

Don't write notes on ruled or inferior paper.
Don't use sheets with business headings for
private letters. Tasteful stationery is considered an indication of refined breeding,

and tasteful stationery means note-paper and envelopes of choice quality, but entirely plain. One may have his initials or his monogram and his address neatly printed on his note-paper, but there should be no ornament of any kind.

Don't—we wish we could say—fasten an envelope by moistening the mucilage with your lips; but this custom is too universally established for a protest against it to be of any avail. No one, however, can defend the practice as altogether nice. It was once incumbent on a gentleman to seal his letters with wax, and many fastidious persons adhered to the practice long after wafers came in. A Frenchman, it is said, once challenged an Englishman for sending him a letter fastened by a

wafer. "What right," exclaimed the punc-
tilious Gaul, "has any gentleman to send
me his saliva ?"

Don't cultivate an ornamental style of writing.
Don't imitate the flourishes of a writing-
master; keep as far away from a writing-
master's style as possible. A lady's or gentleman's handwriting should be perfectly
plain, and wholly free from affectations of
all kinds.

Don't, when you inclose a letter to a correspondent to be forwarded, omit to place a
stamp on the letter.

Don't fail to acknowledge by note all invita-
tions, whether accepted or not. Never
leave a letter unanswered. Don't fail to
acknowledge all courtesies, all attentions, all
kindnesses.

Don't, in writing to a young lady, address her as " Dear Miss." The use of *Miss* without the name is always a vulgarism, if not an impertinence. It is awkward, no doubt, to address a young woman as " Dear Madam," but there is no help for it, unless one makes a rule for himself, and writes, " Dear Lady."

Don't, in writing to a married lady, address her by her Christian name. Don't, for instance, write " Mrs. Lucy Smith," but " Mrs. Charles Smith."

Don't omit from your visiting-cards your title, *Mr.*, *Mrs.*, or *Miss*, whatever it may be. It is very common in the United States for gentlemen to omit *Mr.* from their visiting-cards ; and sometimes young ladies print their names without a title, but

the custom has not the sanction of the best
usage.*

Don't scold your children or your servants before others.   Respect their *amour propre*.

Don't bring children into company.   Don't set
them at table where there are guests.   Don't
force them on people's attention.

Don't, as master or mistress, give your orders
in an authoritative manner.   The feelings of
those under you should be considered.   You
will obtain more willing obedience if your
directions have as little as possible of the
tone of command.

Don't trouble people with your domestic
mishaps, with accounts of your rebell-

---

* In England a young lady does not commonly have a
separate visiting-card ; her name is printed on the card of
her mother, with whom her visits are always made.

ious servants, or with complaints of any kind.

Don't repeat scandals, or malicious gossip. Don't sneer at people, or continually crack jokes at their expense ; cultivate the amenities and not the asperities of life.

Don't be that intolerable torment—a tease. The disposition to worry children, cats, and dogs simply displays the restlessness of an empty mind. Don't chaff.

Don't underrate everything that others do, and overstate your own doings.

Don't scoff or speak ill of a rival in your profession or trade. This is in the worst possible taste, and shows a paltry spirit. Have the pride and self-respect to overstate the merits of a rival rather than understate them.

Don't borrow books unless you return them promptly. If you do borrow books, don't mar them in any way; don't bend or break the backs, don't fold down the leaves, don't write on the margins, don't stain them with grease-spots. Read them, but treat them as friends that must not be abused.

Don't play the accordion, the violin, the piano, or any musical instrument, to excess. Your neighbors have nerves, and need at times a little relief from inflictions of the kind. If you could manage not to play on instruments at all, unless you are an accomplished performer, so much the better.

Don't be selfish; don't be exacting; don't storm, if things go wrong; don't be grum and sullen; don't fret—one fretful person in a house is ruin to its peace; don't make yourself in any particular a nuisance to your neighbors or your family.

Don't fail to heed all the "don'ts" in this little book. Perhaps you think the injunctions are not needed in your case. This is true of many of them, no doubt; but the best of us are not perfect in manners any more than in anything else.

VII.

Affectionately addressed to Womankind.

DON'T over-trim your gowns or other articles of apparel. The excess in trimmings on women's garments, now so common, is a taste little less than barbaric, and evinces ignorance of the first principles of beauty, which always involve simplicity as a cardinal virtue. Apparel piled with furbelows or similar adjuncts, covered with ornaments, and garnished up and down with ribbons, is simply made monstrous thereby, and is not of a nature to please the eyes of gods or men. Leave excesses of all kinds to the vulgar.

Don't use the word *dress* for your outside garment. This is American-English, and, common as it is, has not the sanction of correct speakers or writers. Fortunately, the good old word *gown* is again coming into vogue; indeed, its use is now considered the sign of high-breeding.

Don't submit servilely to fashion. Believe in your own instincts and the looking-glass rather than the *dicta* of the mantua-makers, and modify modes to suit your personal peculiarities. How is it possible for a tall woman and a short woman to wear garments of the same style without one or the other being sacrificed?

Don't forget that no face can be lovely
when exposed to the full glare of the sun.
A bonnet should be so constructed as to
cast the features partially in shade, for the
delicate half-shadows that play in the eyes
and come and go on the cheek give to
woman's beauty one of its greatest charms.
When fashion thrusts the bonnet on the
back of the head, defy it; when it orders
the bonnet to be perched on the nose, refuse to be a victim of its tyranny.

Don't wear at home faded or spotted gowns,
or soiled finery, or anything that is not neat
and appropriate. Appear at the breakfast-
table in some perfectly pure and delicate at-
tire—fresh, cool, and delicious, like a newly-
plucked flower. Dress for the pleasure and
admiration of your family.

Don't cover your fingers with finger-rings. A
few well-chosen rings give elegance and
beauty to the hand ; a great number dis-
figure it, while the ostentation of such a dis-
play is peculiarly vulgar. And what are we
to say when many ringed fingers show a
neglect of the wash-basin ?

Don't wear ear-rings that draw down the lobe
of the ear. A well-shaped ear is a handsome
feature ; but an ear misshapen by the weight
of its trinkets is a thing not pleasant to be-
hold.

Don't wear diamonds in the morning, or to
any extent except upon dress occasions.
Don't wear too many trinkets of any kind.

Don't supplement the charms of nature by the
use of the color-box. Fresh air, exercise,
the morning bath, and proper food, will give

to the cheek nature's own tints, and no other
have any true beauty.

Don't indulge in confections or other sweets.
It must be said that American women devour an immense deal of rubbish. If they
would banish from the table pickles, pre-
serves, pastry, cakes, and similar indigestible
articles, and never touch candy, their appe-
tite for wholesome food would be greatly
increased, and as a consequence we should
see their cheeks blooming like the rose.

Don't permit your voice to be high and
shrill. Cultivate those low and soft tones
which in the judgment of all ages and all
countries constitute one of the charms of
woman.

Don't give yourself wholly to the reading of
novels. An excess of this kind of reading

is the great vice of womankind. Good novels are good things, but how can women
hope to occupy an equal place with men if
their intellectual life is given to one branch
of literature solely?

Don't publicly kiss every time you come together or part. Consider the aggravation
to men, and the waste—and remember that
public displays of affection are in questionable taste.

Don't use terms of endearment when you
do not mean them. The word *dear* in the
mouths of women is often nothing more
than a feminine way of spelling *detestable*.

Don't, on making a call, keep talking about
your departure, proposing to go and not
going. When you are ready to go **say** so
and then depart.

Don't make endless adieux in leaving friends. The woman who begins at the top of the stairs, and overflows with farewells and parting admonitions every step on the way down, and repeats them a hundred times at the door, simply maddens the man who is her escort, be he her husband or lover. Be persuaded, ladies, to say "good-by" once or twice, and have done with it.

Don't forget to thank the man who surrenders his seat in the car or omnibus, or who politely passes up your fare. Sweet thanks from a woman are ample compensation for any sacrifice a man may make in such cases, or any trouble to which he may be put.

Don't carry your parasol or umbrella when closed so as to endanger the eyes of every one who comes near you. Don't, when in a public vehicle, thrust those articles across the passage so as to trip up the heedless or entangle the unwary.

Don't be loud of voice in public places. A retiring, modest demeanor may have ceased to be fashionable, but it is as much a charm in women to-day as it ever was.

Don't nag. The amiability of woman, in view of all they are subjected to from unsympathetic and brutal man, deserves great praise, but sometimes——— Let it not be written !

Don't, young ladies, giggle, or affect merriment when you feel none. If you reward a *bonmot* with a smile, it is sufficient. There are young women who every time they laugh cover their faces with their hands, or indulge in some other violent demonstration—to whom we say, *don't*.

Don't doubt the compiler's admiration for woman. Very few, indeed, are the social shortcomings of women compared with those of men, but the few injunctions here set down may not be unprofitable, and are given with entire respect and good-will.

The
Vellum-Parchment Shilling Series

OF

Miscellaneous Literature.

No. i.

"ENGLISH AS SHE IS SPOKE: OR A JEST IN SOBER EARNEST."
"*Excruciatingly funny.*" — The World.

No. i *a*.

"ENGLISH AS SHE IS SPOKE: OR, A JEST IN SOBER EARNEST."
"HER SECONDS PART." (NEW MATTER.) *As funny as*
the first part.

No. ii.

The Story of a Nursery Rhyme, By C. B.,

with numerous whole-page illustrations, by Edwin J. Ellis. The text,
which is set *entirely* in the very beautiful and artistic type which
heads this notice, and the illustrations, are printed throughout in a
new shade of blue ink.

No. iii.

HENRY IRVING, ACTOR AND MANAGER: A Critical Study. By
WILLIAM ARCHER.

No. iv.

CHRISTMAS ENTERTAINMENTS, illustrated with many diverting
cuts—a reprint of the very amusing and scarce 1740 edition,
an original copy of which would now command more than twice its
weight in gold.

John Bull and his Island. Translated from the French under the supervision of the Author. [*Paper Covers, 2/6 ; Cloth, 3/6.*

Field & Tuer, Yᵉ Leadenhalle Presse, E.C.

Bygone Beauties: "A SELECT SERIES OF TEN PORTRAITS OF LADIES OF RANK AND FASHION," from paintings by John Hoppner, R.A., and engraved by Charles Wilkin; annotated by Andrew W. Tuer. [*Large folio*, 21s.

Quaintly beautiful portraits of beautiful women and eminently adapted for separate framing. Single examples of the original prints fetch at an auction several pounds.

FIELD & TUER, Ye Leadenhalle Presse, E.C.

Amongst the Shans. By Archibald Ross Colquhoun, A.M.I.C.E., F.R.G.S., Author of "Across Chrysê." With upwards of Fifty whole-page Illustrations. Edited by Holt S. Hallett, M.I.C.E., F.R.G.S. [21s.

FIELD & TUER, Ye Leadenhalle Presse, E.C.

The Pyramids and Temples of Gizeh. By W. M. Flinders Petrie. Containing an account of excavations and surveys carried on at Gizeh during 1880-1-2 ; with the application of the results to various modern theories of the pyramids. [*Crown 4to, 250 pp. and 17 plates, price* 18s.

FIELD & TUER, Ye Leadenhalle Presse, E.C.

An Essay of Scarabs. By W. J. Loftie, B.A., F.S.A. (Author of "A History of London.") Together with a Catalogue of Ancient Egyptian Amulets of various kinds, bearing the names of Kings. [21s.

FIELD & TUER, Ye Leadenhalle Presse, E.C.

Collectors' Marks. By Louis Fagan, with Frontispiece by the Author. (For the use of Print Collectors.) [21s.

FIELD & TUER, Ye Leadenhalle Presse, E.C.

Crawhall's Chap-book Chaplets: Adorn'd with suitable Sculptures. *The many hundreds of cuts being all hand-coloured, the issue is necessarily limited.* Contents of the Volume: I. The Barkshire Lady's Garland. II. The Babes in the Wood. III. I know what I know. IV. Jemmy and Nancy of Yarmouth. V. The Taming of a Shrew. VI. Blew-cap for me. VII. John and Joan. VIII. George Barnewel. [*Now ready. In one thick 4to vol.,* 25s.

FIELD & TUER, Ye Leadenhalle Presse, E.C.

London Cries: with Six Charming
Children printed direct from stippled plates
in the Bartolozzi style, and duplicated in red
and brown, and about forty other illustrations,
including ten of Rowlandson's humorous sub-
jects in *facsimile*, and tinted ; examples by
George Cruikshank, Joseph Crawhall, &c., &c.
The text by ANDREW W. TUER, Author of
" Bartolozzi and his Works," &c. LONDON :
Field & Tuer, Ye Leadenhalle Presse, E.C.

One Guinea: Large Paper Signed Proofs (250 only)
Two Guineas : Large Paper Signed Proofs on
Satin (50 only) Four Guineas.

When is your Birthday ? or a
Year of Good Wishes. Set of Twelve Designs
by Edwin J. Ellis, with Sonnets by the Artist.
A beautiful book.   [*Now ready*. 21s.
FIELD & TUER, Ye Leadenhalle Presse, E.C.

Olde ffrendes wyth newe Faces:

Adorn'd with suitable Sculptures. By Joseph Crawhall. *The many hundreds of cuts being all hand-coloured, the issue is necessarily limited.* Table of the Matter herein contained: I. The louing Ballad of Lord Bateman. II. A true relation of the Apparition of Mrs. Veal. III. The Long Pack: A Northumbrian Tale. IV. The Sword Dancers. V. John Cunningham, the Pastoral Poet. VI. Ducks and Green Peas, or the Newcastle Rider: a Tale in Rhyme. VII. Ducks and Green Peas: a Farce. VIII. Andrew Robinson Stoney Bowes, Esquire. IX. The Gloamin' Buchte. [*In one thick 4to vol., 25s.*

FIELD & TUER, Ye Leadenhalle Presse, E.C.

Prince Pertinax:

A Fairy Tale, by Mrs. George Hooper, Authoress of "The House of Raby," "Arbell," &c. Illustrated with Twenty-six drawings in sepia by Margaret L. Hooper and Margery May. *A charming present.* [*Now ready.* 21s.

FIELD & TUER, Ye Leadenhalle Presse, E.C.

MORE FACSIMILE REISSUES
FROM PRYOR PUBLICATIONS

Old London Street Cries

'A beautiful pocket-sized facsimile, complete with *faux marbre* cover, lovely thick cream paper and cream ribbons to keep it shut . . . provides a brief history, an essay on cockney pronunciation and an index of street cries, in addition to the superb little engravings of street vendors and their cries.' *London Evening Standard.*

First published 1885   156 pages   over 50 woodcuts
hardback   ISBN: 0 946014 00 0   **£7.**95

Everybody's Book of Correct Conduct
Being the Etiquette of Everyday Life

'It is certain that he who lives correctly every day will find himself following the higher laws of morality and rectitude.'

First published 1893   192 pages
ISBN: 0 946014 37 X   paperback   **£4.**99

A SHORT HISTORY OF THE WOLF IN BRITAIN

Taken from James Harting's 'British Animals Extinct Within Modern Times', first published in 1880, here are early accounts of the wolf in the British Isles until its demise around 1760.
96 pages   Illustrated   ISBN: 0 946014 27 2   Paperback   **£5.**95

MANNERS FOR MEN

Mrs Humphry, who is also the author of *Manners for Women*, wrote 'Like every other woman I have my ideal of manhood. The difficulty is to describe it. First of all, he must be a gentleman, but that means so much that it, in its turn, requires explanation . . .'

First published 1897   176 pages
ISBN: 0 946014 23 X   *Paperback*

£4.⁵⁰

MANNERS FOR WOMEN

Can anything be nicer than a really nice girl? 'may seem quaint but it is a useful reminder that tittering is an unpleasant habit and curtseying should be avoided unless you know what you are doing.' *The Times.*

First published 1897   164 pages
ISBN: 0 946014 17 5   *Paperback*

£4.⁵⁰

A PLAIN COOKERY BOOK FOR THE WORKING CLASSES

Charles Elme Francatelli, Late Maitre d'Hotel and chief cook to Her Gracious Majesty Queen Victoria

'My object in writing this little book is to show you how you may prepare and cook your daily food, so as to obtain from it the greatest amount of nourishment at the least possible expense, and thus, by skill and economy, add, at the same time, to your comfort and to your comparatively slender means.' Charles Elme Francatelli.

Contains over 240 recipes, including 'Baked Bullocks Hearts', 'Sheep Pluck', 'Cow Meal Broth' and 'Rice Gruel, a Remedy for Relaxed Bowels.' There are also sections on Cookery and Diet for the Sick Room and Economical and Substantial Soup for the Poor.

Originally published 1861. Size 14.9cm x 10.4cm
112 Pages Paperback. ISBN 0 946014 15 9

£4.⁰⁰

THE NATURAL HISTORY OF STUCK-UP PEOPLE

ALBERT SMITH

'We are about to expose, as simply and truthfully as we can, the foolish conventionalities of a large proportion of the middle classes of the present day, who believe that position is attained by climbing up a staircase of moneybags.' Delightfully illustrated.

Originally published 1847. · Size 13cm x 10.5cm

128 Pages Paperback, Illustrated. ISBN 0 946014 39 6   £4.00

Albert Smith was one of the greatest showmen of the 19th century. His entertainments were as popular a feature of the capital as Madame Tussaud's and the Tower of London. This book was one of a series of fictionalised accounts that were very popular with Victorian readers.

EVERYBODY'S BOOK OF EPITAPHS

Being For The Most Part What The Living Think Of The Dead

Here lies my wife, a sad slattern and shrew
If I said I regretted her, I should lie too!

A look at epitaphs for the famous to the poor — some amusing, some sad, some historic, some enlightening, all fascinating.

Here lies John Wherdle, Parish Beedle
Who was so very knowing
His wisdom's gone, and so is he,
Because he left off growing.

Originally published 1885. Size 13.5cm x 10.5cm

128 Pages Paperback. ISBN 0 946014 38 8   £4.50

A full list of our publications sent on request. All books post and packing free.

PRYOR PUBLICATIONS
75 Dargate Road, Yorkletts, Whitstable, Kent CT5 3AE.
Tel/Fax: (01227) 274655